Worthy Is the Lamb

Charles R. Swindoll

INSIGHT FOR LIVING

WORTHY IS THE LAMB

ACKNOWLEDGMENTS

This booklet was adapted by Insight for Living staff from the original sermon and outline titled "Worthy Is the Lamb" from the sermon series, *Revelation—Unveiling the End, Act 1*, plus unpublished teaching material from Charles R. Swindoll. Copyright © 2003, 2006, 2024 by Charles R. Swindoll, Inc.

President, Insight for Living: Charissa Swindoll Gaither
Senior Vice President, Communications and Engagement: Linda Ricks, BBA, Baylor University
Senior Vice President, *Searching the Scriptures* Ministries: Aaron Massey, ThM, Dallas Theological Seminary
Vice President, *Searching the Scriptures* Ministries: Bryce Klabunde, ThM, Dallas Theological Seminary; DMin, Western Seminary
Project Manager, Publishing: Haley Hulkenberg, Certified Associate in Project Management (CAPM), Project Management Institute
Print Communications Manager: Autumn Swindoll, BA, Humanities, Biola University
Production Editor: Katie Hayes, BA, Communications, Southwest Baptist University
Substantive Editor: Jim Craft, MA, English, Mississippi College; MA, Christian Studies, Dallas Theological Seminary
Designer: Laura Dubroc, BFA, Advertising Design, University of Louisiana at Lafayette
Production Artist: Nancy Gustine, BFA, Advertising Art, University of North Texas

Printed in the United States of America

Worthy Is the Lamb

A Note from Charissa

In Psalm 91, David masterfully illustrates a profound image of shelter and safety, capturing the essence of God as a refuge for His people. He begins with a gentle invitation, beckoning us to "find rest in the shadow of the Almighty." This is no ordinary haven; it is an intimate sanctuary where we can lay down our burdens and find security in the unyielding embrace of our Creator.

Every time I hear, "Worthy Is the Lamb" I imagine a gentle lamb in a grassy field with mountains in the distance. There is a serene feeling that gives me complete peace. I felt that same peaceful serenity when Pastor Chuck shared his devotional at our board of director's meeting. Because it was so inspiring, we wanted everyone to hear what he said. You are holding that devotional in your hands.

In times of turmoil, we frantically search for solace, a quest that too often leaves us feeling lost and alone. Yet, this passage reminds us that we can find authentic peace when we choose to draw close to God—sheltering under the protective "shadow of the Most High." How comforting to remember that while He does not promise a life free from trouble, He does assure us of His abiding presence as we confront life's challenges.

As you read Chuck's words, remember that Christ is the One we turn to in times of suffering and uncertainty. As you read, you will discover that Chuck had many challenging experiences of his own, and the people the Lord provided along the way to encourage him changed the course of his life.

Charissa Swindoll Gaither
President
Insight for Living

Worthy Is the Lamb

It was fall 1971.

The waning glow of dusk had long past vanished into a blanket of night. I was still at my desk at church. All the staff had gone home, and I was alone in the quiet. Just a few months earlier, I had been called to serve as pastor of this church. Cynthia and I had bundled up our four young children, packed up everything we owned, and moved from our home in Texas to far-off and unknown Fullerton, California.

This was the fourth church I had served since graduating from Dallas Theological Seminary eight years earlier in 1963. I would pastor this church—the First Evangelical Church of Fullerton—for the next 23 years, but I had no clue what the future would hold. I was staring into the thick curtain of uncertainty. Frankly, I was at a low point in my ministry. For all I knew, this pastorate would be no different from my previous experiences. Minimal growth, no tangible impact, and short-lived.

Just then, the shrill ring of my desk phone pierced the quiet. I smiled when I heard the familiar voice of my long-time friend, musician, and composer Don Wyrtzen. He was at his home in Nashville sitting at his piano, and he had just finished a composition that really moved him.

He said, "Chuck, I want you to be the first to hear this." As soon as he began playing, I closed my eyes and leaned back in my chair and just listened. The lyrics were taken from Revelation 5:12. I had just memorized the verse several weeks earlier in my Scripture memory program. He elevated both of us into a majestic scene of worship in Revelation 4–5 with these words:

> Worthy is the Lamb that was slain.
> Worthy is the Lamb that was slain.
> Worthy is the Lamb that was slain.
>
> To receive power and riches
> And wisdom and strength,
> Honor and glory and blessing!
>
> Worthy is the Lamb,
> Worthy is the Lamb
> Worthy is the Lamb that was slain.
> Worthy is the Lamb![1]

Without another word, without another note, he just simply hung up. In the words of hymnwriter Charles Wesley, I found myself "lost in wonder, love, and praise." I teared up realizing that, although Don didn't know it, he had just provided me with the theme for my life.

Worthy Is the Lamb

From that point on, my life in ministry would, by God's grace, be marked with these four words, *worthy is the Lamb*. Whatever the future held, my sole purpose was to glorify the One who was worthy of praise. All power, riches, wisdom, strength, honor, glory, and blessing belong to Him and Him alone!

I can't tell you the weight that lifted from my shoulders when I realized my job was simply to worship Christ, serve Him, and leave the results with Him. All it takes is a glimpse of Christ's majesty to lift my spirit out of the pit and energize me to the core. My life is one small light among millions all reflecting the glory of Christ. Everything I have done is through His enablement, by His grace, and for His glory. None of it is of my own strength—as you'll see as I share more of my story.

A Testament to God's Grace

Up until that day in fall 1971, I had known almost no success in ministry. No growth in any church. No written works that people were quoting. Nothing of notoriety at all. In 1963, I was honored to be asked by Dr. J. Dwight Pentecost to be his first assistant pastor. I just couldn't believe he would invite me to do that. Dr. Pentecost was one of the most well-known expositors in the world. When he spoke, people stayed quiet, took notes, and listened. His books would fly off the shelves and into the hands of Christians around the world. He was very popular, though he never sought that. I assured him I would be honored to be his assistant.

I was an absolute no-name novice, and, of all things, Dr. Pentecost said to me, "Now, when I'm not here, I want you to fill the pulpit." I still remember the squiggles, I call them, that happened in my stomach when he said that because I couldn't imagine preaching behind his pulpit. The Saturday before I preached for him for the first time, I was all alone at the church, and I stepped behind the pulpit to see if I'd be turning into a crisp from the lightning of God for even standing there.

Mine was a borrowed popularity. I'm sure that there were those who came to Grace Bible Church during the years I was there, who were often disappointed as they came to hear this well-spoken, brilliant expositor, only to wind up hearing a guy named "Swindle" doing his best to preach, trying my best to be myself and not a clone of his, which would be impossible.

I said to him often, "Wouldn't you like to use someone else?" He would say, "No, I want you to be the one who preaches when I'm not here." I said, "Well, maybe you want that, but from the faces I look at out in front of me, there are not a lot of others that would agree with you." He said, "You just do as I ask."

In 1965, we decided it was time for us to leave my role under Dr. Pentecost. I accepted a call to pastor a church in Waltham, Massachusetts, so we moved the family from Texas to New England. The two years there were of some of the toughest years I've ever known in ministry.

The Toughest Years

These years were *tough* because New England is not only a location, but it's a way of life. If you don't pick up the way of life, you don't mix well with the people. And we didn't. I felt like a misfit from the day I drove onto Bruce Road, where the small church was located.

I remember Cynthia's first words when we got on the road leading to the church, "This is it?" The church was tucked back off the thoroughfare, and you had to really want to find the church to find it. And then when you found it, you had to listen to me preach.

The people were gracious, but I did a poor job there. I remember one summer day we had, I think, seven or eight in the congregation, and four of them were Swindolls. So, it wasn't a church overflowing with people interested in the one filling the pulpit.

One day, a man from a bedroom community outside of Dallas phoned and said, "I'm representing Irving Bible Church, and we have just lost our pastor." He didn't tell me who he was. Later, I found out it was Dr. Stan Toussaint, one of my beloved former professors. I told him I was a little reluctant to know how to respond, but I would pray about it. Cynthia's response was immediate: "You can pray while I pack." She was already on her way! I was reluctant because I don't think I was ready for another failure, but Cynthia knew best, and we accepted the position.

So, in 1967, we returned to Texas where I began pastoring Irving Bible Church. I didn't realize when I took the church at Irving that it was the result of a split, and most of the disgruntled people from the split found their way into this little church. It was a challenging place to serve, but we did our best.

An Unexpected Call

Then, one cold day—February 9, 1971 to be precise—my phone rang at home in Texas. It was a man named John Watson from a place called Fullerton, California. He said to me, "We just had Hadden Robinson here, and before him was Bruce Waltke, and both of them mentioned you as a possible candidate for our church to be a pastor."

I couldn't believe the timing of his call. You can't make it up. Earlier that day, I had received the news that my mother had just died. It was not a good time, and that was not a good day. Of course, John didn't know that. He apologized. I said, "Really, I'm not ready for a move. I'd just gotten started here, and I've only been here four years. I feel there's much more to be done."

He said, "Well, may I call you back?" I said, "Well, you can do whatever you want to do, John, but I'm not coming."

He did call and was very gracious. He offered to bring us out for a vacation, the whole family. By then, we had four children. They were all small and still in elementary school or not even in school yet. I had heard all the warnings about the free-wheeling California lifestyle, and I could only imagine what it would be like to live there.

We finally accepted the call. We went because I believed the Lord was in all of this, even though one person after another objected. In fact, while we were in our car ready to make the drive to California, one lady leaned into our open car window and said, "The Lord gets blamed for a lot of things He has nothing to do with." That was our sendoff from the church in Texas, another place where I would call a failure.

Surprised by Grace

I was brand new as pastor of the church in Fullerton when Don Wyrtzen called me in fall 1971. I had no notoriety. I'd written no books—never even thought of doing such a thing. I was certainly not on the radio, and I had no interest in that endeavor—much less plans for it. As time passed, God had other arrangements for me.

I was the most surprised of all when growth occurred at our church. It was far beyond what anyone in the church or any of us who served on staff ever expected. We grew and grew and grew and kept adding services until we were doing five services a Sunday.

In the middle of all of that, I preached a sermon one Sunday night, titled, "For Those Who Hurt." A man in our congregation, who was really hurting because his daughter had run away, came up to me and he said, "What you have just preached needs to be in print."

I said, "Well, I'll be glad to mimeograph my sermon for you." He said, "No, no, no . . . I mean in a book." I said, "No, I'm not a writer, and I'm not going to put this in a book." He said, "I'll pay for whatever needs to be paid for." I said, "I don't even know if you have to pay to write for someone but thank you. Save your money. I'll run you off a copy of my sermon." I mentioned that to my secretary the next morning, who said to me, "I'll be glad to type it and you'll have at least a manuscript."

I was getting ready to go to Dallas Seminary to celebrate the jubilee anniversary, and I thought, *I might run into a publisher there.* I'd taken a manuscript to four different publishers, and they weren't interested. I didn't blame them. I was a nobody, and this was my first attempt at writing for publication. Finally, at this conference at the seminary, I met up with John Van Diest, who happened to be the publisher at Multnomah Press. I said to John, "You may look at this." I said to myself, *If he says no, that's it, I'm not going any further.*

He looked at it and read it and the next morning he said, "We'd love to publish this." I replied, "You're kidding. You want to publish it?" I was almost ready to talk him out of it. He said, "We'll make it into a gift book." I couldn't believe it. Before I knew it, Thomas Nelson got hold of me and wanted to do three books, and here I was in the midst of a growing ministry I was hardly able to keep up with.

All along I was remembering that *the Lamb alone is worthy.* Whatever I write is for God's glory. Whatever I preach is for the glory of God. The Lamb who was slain gets all the glory.

All for God's Glory

I was now in the midst of a writing ministry that I never wanted or planned for. I never took one lesson in how to write.

To my amazement, people were reading what I was writing. I kept saying to Cynthia, "This is unbelievable. They want another book."

John Van Diest said to me one day, "You need a crossover publisher, one that will put your books on the secular market as well as the Christian."

I had met a couple of men from Word Books, and I thought, *Well maybe they'd be interested*. That's about the time I wrote a little book called *Improving Your Serve*. I mean, it took off. The men from Word Books said to me, "We've never had a book do this." In my heart, I thought, *Worthy is the Lamb that was slain*.

In the late 1970s, radio producer Al Sanders kept bugging me about broadcasting, and I couldn't say no fast enough. I said, "N . . . O . . ." He kept pushing me and he said, "You know, it won't take much of your time." *Right*.

I finally agreed when Cynthia said she would be the one who would lead it. I never wanted to be on the radio. Never planned a worldwide ministry. I'm the most reluctant leader you could ever want to meet. Publishers wanted more books, and now this broadcasting ministry, *Insight for Living*, began to take off. The church wouldn't stop growing. The number of people coming to church on Sundays was causing problems for the neighbors, and they wouldn't stop complaining. We were parking all over their yards and driveways.

I remember I was preaching on Noah, and I got to the part where he was going to build the ark. I decided to go out with a tape measure and mark off the measurements of an ark. I was in the parking lot doing that, and I felt like a shadow was behind me at the time. I looked around, and it was one of our neighbors who was already mad at me.

He said, "Who are you?" I said, "I'm the pastor of this church." "I thought so," he retorted. "What are you doing?" I said, "Well, I'm measuring Noah's Ark out here."

He said, "You're not getting ready to build one of *those things* are you?"

I said, "No, no, no. No, sir, we're not going to build an ark out here." But that was sort of testimony in the neighborhood since we had broken all the rules for good neighbors. We didn't stop growing even when we moved into the new building. And those services were packed. But all along the way, my thought was, *Worthy is the Lamb*. This declaration must remain the theme of my life—regardless of how little or how much the Lord decides to use me.

That's your life purpose, too—to glorify the Lamb that was slain. Together as the body of Christ, we get to do now what we will do for eternity. We get a head-start in joining the myriads of angels worshiping the Lamb. The apostle John tells us about our glorious future with Christ in the book of Revelation. Let's take a peek at what's in store.

A Thrilling Glimpse into the Future

Revelation, or the Apocalypse (unveiling) as it is called in Greek, is John's record of Christ's revelation to him regarding "the events that must soon take place" (Revelation 1:1). Caught up in the vision, John heard a voice inviting him into heaven where he saw God as a resplendent figure sitting on a throne (Revelation 4–5).

A brilliant light emanated from the figure, and a radiant glow encircled His throne like a rainbow. Twenty-four elders dressed in white sat on twenty-four thrones that surrounded the throne of God. Lightning flashed and thunder rumbled as John witnessed four magnificent six-winged creatures flying overhead proclaiming with booming voices:

> *"Holy, holy, holy is the Lord God, the*
> *Almighty—*
> *the one who always was, who is,*
> *and who is to come."* (4:8)

John noticed in God's right hand a seven-sealed scroll. In ancient times, sealed scrolls like these were legal documents declaring ownership. Only the rightful heir could open the document and receive the inheritance. This scroll was God's blueprint for restoring His creation. It contained the actions required to right all wrongs and renew the world to its original design. Only the one who was worthy could receive creation as an inheritance and perform the duties written in the scroll. But who was worthy? Who was qualified to be the ultimate judge of humankind and the king of all creation?

The hope of the world was written in this scroll! Wasn't there anyone worthy to open it? Who was capable of ushering in a new day of righteousness and justice in our dark and broken world?

No one in heaven or on earth could be found, and so John "began to weep bitterly" (Revelation 5:4). The tears of the victims and the brokenhearted through the ages poured from his heart. At that moment, all hope seemed lost.

But then one of the elders spoke:

> *"Stop weeping! Look, the Lion of the tribe of Judah, the heir to David's throne, has won the victory. He is worthy to open the scroll and its seven seals."* (5:5)

Appearing before John was the worthy One. Only, instead of a powerful Lion, John "saw a Lamb that looked as if it had been slaughtered" (5:6). The four heavenly creatures and the twenty-four elders fell before the Lamb that was slain. This Lamb was no weakling. Besides His wounds, John saw that:

> *He had seven horns and seven eyes, which represent the sevenfold Spirit of God that is sent into every part of the earth.* (Revelation 5:6)

His magnificent horns and many eyes bore witness to the Lamb's mighty power and His sovereign rule. He was the *omnipotent* and *omniscient* One who reigned over creation . . . but who had taken on the form of a Lamb to bear sin's curse and save the world.

The elders held a harp in one hand as they offered gold incense bowls filled with "the prayers of God's people" (5:8)—yes, even your prayers! They sang in praise of the Lamb and what His sacrifice accomplished.

The Lamb's blood had ransomed souls "from every tribe and language and people and nation" for God (5:9). That's us! Why did Christ redeem us? To give us a new identity—to make us into "a Kingdom of priests for our God"—and a grand purpose—to one day "reign on the earth" (5:10).

Then the floodgates of praise flung open as millions of angels joined the creatures and the elders and lifted their voices in a mighty chorus:

> "*Worthy is the Lamb who was*
> *slaughtered—to receive power*
> *and riches*
> *and wisdom and strength*
> *and honor and glory and*
> *blessing.*" (Revelation 5:12)

But that's not all! "Every creature in heaven and on earth and under the earth and in the sea" joined the chorus to sing praise to our Savior:

> "*Blessing and honor and glory and power belong to the one sitting on the throne and to the Lamb forever and ever.*" (5:13)

Don Wyrtzen singing these lines over the phone transported in my spirit to this magnificent vision from Revelation 5. Looking back over all that God has accomplished in my lifetime, I bow my head in wonder and praise. *Worthy is the Lamb!*

The Future Can Be Now

In his 90s, Dr. Pentecost requested that he wanted me, of all people, to officiate his memorial service when the Lord took him home. I wondered, *What can I say that could possibly be an appropriate word for Dwight Pentecost, the man who had loved me when I was nothing?*

So, when he passed into the Lord's presence sometime later and the day came for me to prepare the memorial service, I couldn't figure out how to wind things up, how to end it. I pulled his book, *Things to Come*, off the shelf, and I turned toward the end of it and found Dr. Pentecost's favorite hymn. When I read it, I wept. This is the way to close this service. Here are the lyrics to this wonderful hymn. Read them as your own prayer to the Lamb who was slain.

> The sands of time are sinking;
> The dawn of heaven breaks;
> The summer morn I've sighed for,
> The fair sweet morn, awakes;
> Dark, dark has been the midnight,
> But dayspring is at hand,
> And glory, glory dwelleth
> In Emmanuel's land. . . .

O Christ, He is the fountain,
The deep, sweet well of love!
The streams on earth I've tasted;
More deep I'll drink above:
There, to an ocean fullness
His mercy doth expand,
And glory, glory dwelleth
In Emmanuel's land.

The bride eyes not her garment,
But her dear bridegroom's face;
I will not gaze at glory,
But on my King of grace;
Not at the crown He giveth,
But on His pierced hands;
The Lamb is all the glory
Of Emmanuel's land.[2]

I was so grateful to find that piece and have since committed it to memory. It's a wonderful reminder of where the glory goes. You and I must never, ever forget that. We can taste our future before God's heavenly throne now as we live every day to bring glory to the Lamb who was slain.

In whatever way God may use you, *the Lamb gets all the praise!* He's the one who was slain. He's the one who paid the price. He's the one who died that we could live, and who lives that we might know how to die and then live forever.

Heavenly Father,

I'm so grateful, for Your grace in the challenges of today with all its heartaches as well as blessings. Thank You. Thank You for sovereignly controlling our lives. Thank You for never abandoning us but staying with us. "Weeping may endure for the night, but joy comes in the morning." Thank You for Your Son. Thank You for our lifetime of undeserved grace. We worship the Lamb together who alone is worthy to be praised. In the glorious, praiseworthy name of Christ, amen.

Endnotes

1. Don Wyrtzen, "Worthy Is the Lamb" in *The Celebration Hymnal: Songs and Hymns for Worship* (n.p.: Word Music/Integrity Music, 1997), hymn 303.

2. A. R. Cousin, "The Sands of Time Are Sinking," Hymnary.org, hymnary.org/text/the_sands_of_time_are_sinking.